MIRACLE ON THE HUDSON

MIRACLE ON THE HUDSON

WRITTEN &
ILLUSTRATED
by CAROLYN MACY

Dedicated to my family, friends and Captain Chesley Sullenberger with his expertise.

Miracle on the Hudson
Copyright © 2017 by Carolyn Macy. All rights reserved.

No part of this publication may be reproduced, stored in a retrieval system or transmitted in any way by any means, electronic, mechanical, photocopy, recording or otherwise without the prior permission of the author except as provided by USA copyright law.

Published by Carolyn Macy
6227 81st Avenue N.E. | Norman, Oklahoma 73026 USA
405.401.2012

Book design copyright © 2017 by Carolyn Macy.
Written and Illustrated by Carolyn Macy

Published in the United States of America
ISBN: 978-0-9988838-3-0
1. JUVENILE NONFICTION / Biography & Autobiography / Historical
2. JUVENILE NONFICTION / Transportation / Aviation

The Captain and his crew,
  Aboard Flight Fifteen Forty-Nine,
Prepared those folks for flight,
  Then taxied to the take-off line.

Now flying upward in the sky
To leave the airport just behind,
There Captain Sully flew his craft
With course for flight assigned.

As things sometimes do come to pass,
A flock of geese did fly

Into the path flown by the plane
And struck it in the sky.

Their strike made both the engines quit
Which caused the plane to slow,
And glide on from that moment
Over skyline just below.

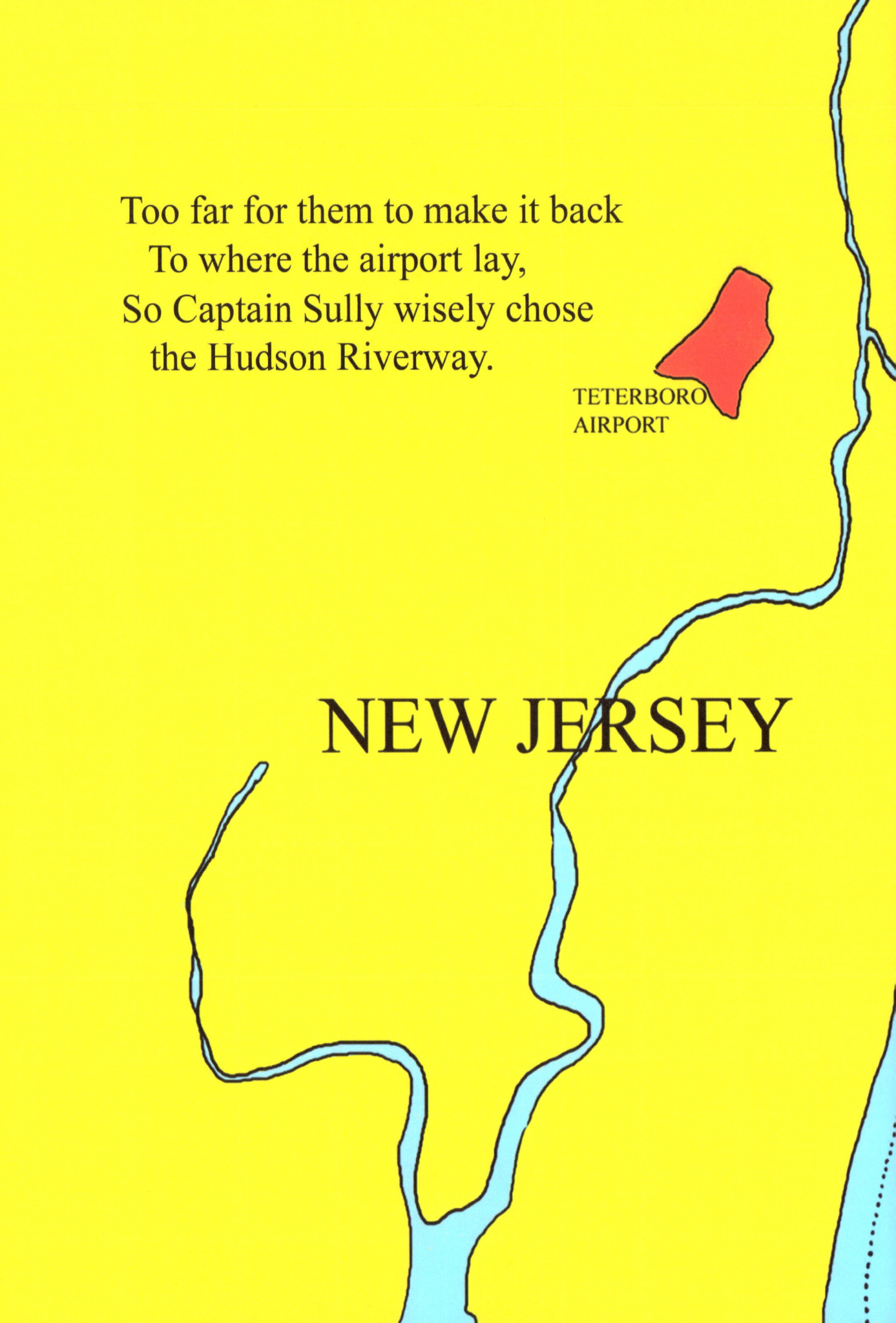

Too far for them to make it back
 To where the airport lay,
So Captain Sully wisely chose
 the Hudson Riverway.

Still fastened in their seats
　With watchful worry while they wait,
　Those folks grabbed life vests to be worn
　With little hurry to inflate.

Now heading for their river stop
With hopes of landing whole,

All those aboard sat calmly braced
And praying for their soul.

Just gliding with the wings held straight,
The nose raised up, but not too much,
And flaps turned down to slow the craft,
He made the tail the first to touch.

He landed on the Hudson
After splashing to a stop
And landed safely in one piece
From their untimely drop.

The pilot, Captain Sully,
In his craft with crew of five
And all one hundred fifty souls
Survived to land alive!

The river showed good will
To all those there that day
Who slowly floated down
Its chilly waterway.

Their rescue by near ferryboats,
  Those folks now numb with cold,
Were seen by some on shore
  Who watched it all unfold.

www.ingramcontent.com/pod-product-compliance
Lightning Source LLC
Chambersburg PA
CBHW041126300426
44113CB00002B/77